Wordcraft

Book One

HELEN ARNOLD

COLLINS EDUCATIONAL

Contents

- These symbols show the author's suggestions for the numbers of children involved.

Unit 1. Listening

People use this all the time.

They use it for eating,
for smiling,
for laughing,
but most of all they use it for **talking.**

Some people talk so much that they
do not wait to see if anyone is **listening.**

Some people never
listen
to anyone else.

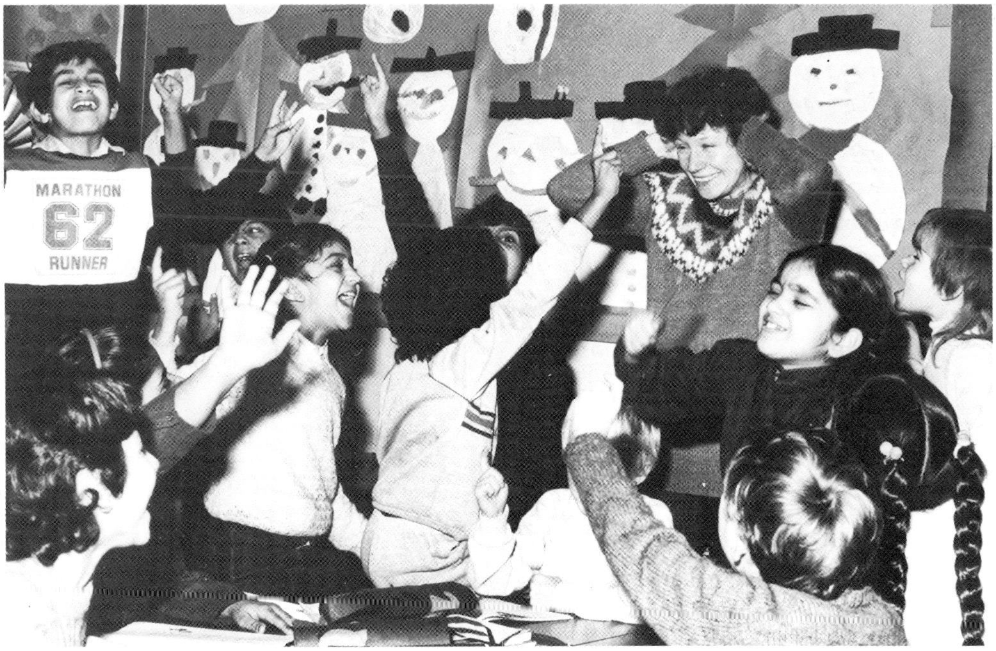

It is easy to tell if someone is **talking** because sounds come out of their mouths.
It is hard to tell if someone is **listening** because there are no sounds.

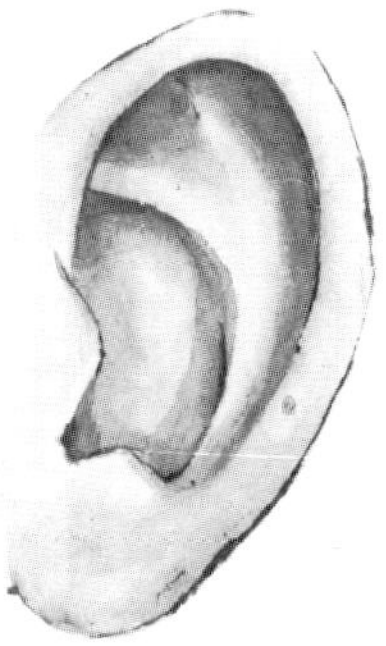

Listening is just as important as **talking.**

Do you listen? Prick up your ears and we'll see.

Babies learn to talk by listening. They listen to all the sounds around them, and they listen to the noises that they make themselves.

They hear things said to them over and over again. Then they try them out by saying them for themselves.

Of course they can't read or write, and they do not know what the words look like. They use words, but they don't know what they are. They hear the words all joined together.

This is what a baby might hear.

- You know what the words are. Can you write out what the baby heard?

Leave the proper spaces between the words.

• • Get some paper and a pencil each.

Shut your eyes and listen hard to all the noises around you – not the talking, but other noises.

When you have heard four different noises, open your eyes.

Write down the four different sounds that you heard.

Like this

a door shutting
an aeroplane

Now see if you have got the same sounds as your friend.

Talk about the sounds. If you heard a door shut, did it make a bang or a click? Was the noise loud or soft? Did you like the noise or not?

LISTENING TO TEACHER

Read this little play. Mrs Brown, the teacher, is talking to the class.

Mrs Brown Today we are going to talk about your pets. How many children in the class have got pets? What is your pet, John?

John I've got a hamster.

Peter (calls out) I've got a hamster too, Miss.

Mrs Brown Don't call out, Peter. And don't call me 'Miss'. My name is Mrs Brown, as you know.
Put your hands up, if you own a hamster.
(Children put up their hands)
Now we know that six children have hamsters.
What do you give your hamster to eat, Mary?

Mary I get special hamster food from the shop.

Mrs Brown Fine. Now I want you to write about your pets. Open your books, please. Start on a new line. Don't forget to write neatly.

Copy the passage below. Fill in the gaps. You can find out from the play what Mrs Brown said.

WHAT MRS BROWN SAID

Mrs Brown asked some questions. They were
1.
2.
3.
Mrs Brown told the children what to do.

She gave them some orders. Write down three of her orders.

1.
2.
3.

Mrs Brown said some things which told the children what they must not do. Write three of these.

1.
2.
3.

- Listen very carefully to what your teacher says today.
  Before you go home see if you can write down

  three questions she asked,
  three things that she told the class to do,
  three things that she told the class not to do.

THE WHISPERING GAME

Six children stand in a row. The first one thinks of a message. It might be something like, 'I have got an apple and a banana for my dinner'. Whisper it to the second person. The second person whispers it to the third, and so on down the line. The last person says the message out loud. Has it changed?
The longer the message is, the more it may get changed.
Your are not allowed to ask for the message to be said twice.

THE MESSAGE

A lady called Pat Hutchins wrote a story about a message that went wrong. This is how it starts.

> "I'm having a party tomorrow," whispered Rabbit. "It's a surprise."
> "Rabbit is hoeing the parsley tomorrow," whispered Owl. "It's a surprise."
> "Rabbit is going to sea tomorrow," whispered Squirrel. "It's a surprise."
> "Rabbit is climbing a tree tomorrow," whispered Duck. "It's a surprise."
> "Rabbit is riding a flea tomorrow," whispered Mouse. "It's a surprise."
> "Rabbit is raiding the poultry tomorrow," whispered Fox. "It's a surprise."
> "Reading poetry?" said Frog to himself.

Can you make a list of the words which the animals heard wrongly?

Do it like this.
First, what happened to the word having?
Copy the list and fill in what each animal said.

Having (Rabbit)
_______ (Owl)
_______ (Squirrel)
_______ (Duck)
_______ (Mouse)
_______ (Fox)
Reading (Frog)

What happened to the word party?

Party (Rabbit)
_____ (Owl)
_____ (Squirrel)
_____ (Duck)
_____ (Mouse)
_____ (Fox)
Poetry (Frog)

Look at the parts of the words that went wrong, and what stayed the same. Can you put circles round the letters that got changed? Do it like this

h o e i n g **p a r s l e y**

The animals in the story were very pleased when they found out what Rabbit had really said. You can read what happened if you get the book. Can you guess what the book is called? It is called 'The Surprise Party'.

SOUNDS

Take some paper and a pencil to bed with you tonight. When you wake up tomorrow morning, listen for the very first sound that you hear. Then write down

1. What the sound was,
2. Something about it. Was it loud, soft, gentle, frightening?

What did you think when you heard it?
You might have thought something like,
'I must get up now'.
or 'That's Mum getting the breakfast'.
or 'Dad must be in a good mood today'.

Many, many years ago, two men in Japan woke up very early in the morning, and they wrote down what they heard. The first man wrote,

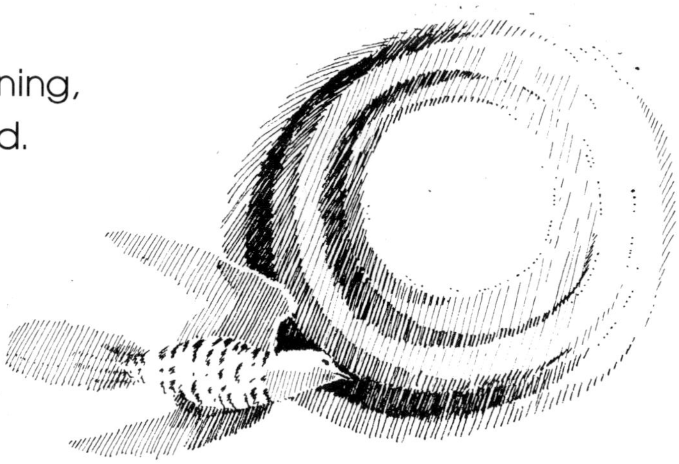

Summer night –
I close my eyes
And the cuckoo
With its one cry
Marks the dawn.

The second man, years later, wrote,

Is it a shower of rain?
I thought as I listened
From my bed, just awake.
But it was falling leaves
Which could not stand the wind.

Bring your notes to school and try to make a poem with your sounds. It could be like this:

Winter night –
I close my eyes
And the wind
With its wooshing
Marks the dawn.

Or like this:

Is it a letter through the door?
I thought as I listened
From my bed, just awake.
But it was the milkman's clatter
As he fell over the sleepy cat.

Unit 2. Observing and recording

Do you know how to use these?
You see thousands of things every day.
Do you look at them carefully?

We shall see!

- Copy the pictures and the table.

Fill in the names: A ball   A needle   A fire

	Name	Words about the thing

Now read the words underneath. They tell you more about the things. The words are all mixed up, though. Pick out the words or groups of words which tell you about each thing. Fill them in on the table in the right spaces.

JUMBLED DESCRIBING WORDS

made of rubber
has a hole in it
round
thin
for sewing
it flickers
sharp
warming
it pricks
made of steel
bounces
can be thrown
hot
dangerous

Can you add some more words of your own?

• • With a friend choose one of these pictures. It might be the clue to a mystery. You must be able to tell about it exactly. Jot down everything you can about it without your friend seeing.
Like this.

Light brown
Hard china
Lid with a knob
Handle
Broken spout
Round

There are many more things you could say about the *teapot*.

• • When you have made your list, look at your friend's. Who has got most? Score 1 point for anything you have written down which is the same as your friend's. Score 2 points if you have got something different. Who won?

RICHARD JEFFRIES AND HIS NOTEBOOKS

Richard Jeffries lived over a hundred years ago. He liked to jot down notes about what he saw. He filled up 24 notebooks. They all had red leather covers. They were very small, exactly the same size as the drawing.

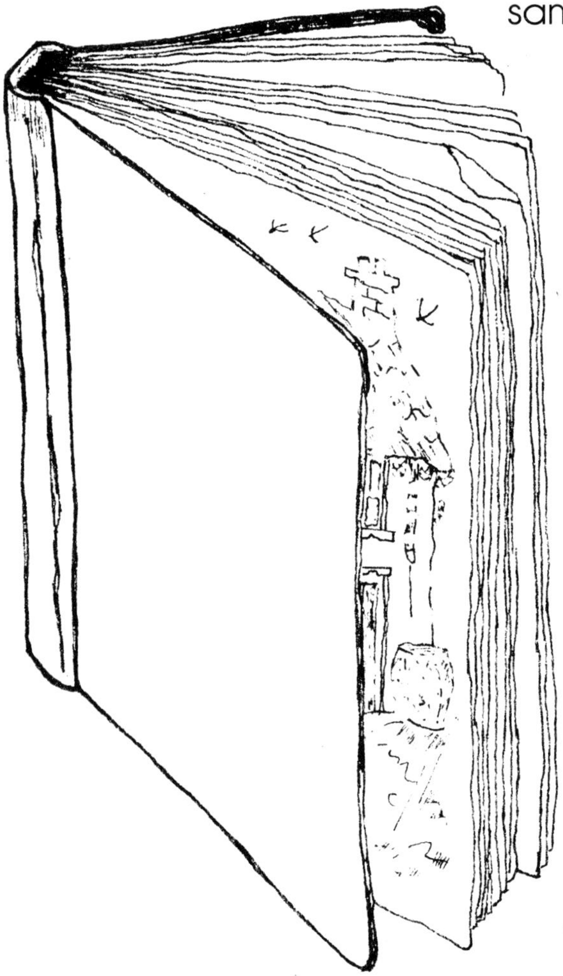

They were easy to put in his pocket.
They were always ready for him to jot down what he saw.
He could look back if he needed to remember anything.
He wrote in pencil.
He did not have to write neatly, as the notebooks were just for himself.
He sometimes made little drawings to help him remember the things.
Later he often turned his notes into stories for people to read.

YOUR NOTEBOOK

Carry it about with you everywhere, and jot down whatever you feel like. Watch out for some of the things Richard Jeffries noticed. They were mostly from the countryside where he lived. There are just as many things to notice in a town.

SOME OF THE THINGS THAT RICHARD JEFFRIES

WROTE DOWN IN HIS NOTEBOOKS

February 1878 – July 1879
Thistledown – enough collected to make a pillow – beautifully soft.

Cat climbing up and getting partly into straw-rick – mice.

Wood-pile – rats – birds' nests – under damp log, lizard.

People never do see things close around them.

The old house, deserted. Wall scribblings. The swallows building inside the broken window, attaching their nests to the ceiling.

Shepherd whistling through his teeth to the sheep.

How far are the birds' notes to be heard? Cuckoo three-quarter mile? I think so as it, the cuckoo, fond of an echo.

Squirrel's tail looks so light because the light passes through its loose delicate fur.

A dog gradually comes out of the water with its tail hung low, for a few yards, before shaking itself.

Butterfly, colour of red velvet.

Moth and wasp on ground fighting – moth got away.

Cat. Kettle boiling. Look on cat's face as if to say 'Tea will be ready in a moment.'

Baby. Turning round before sitting on carpet like a dog.

1. Make a list of the noises which Richard noticed. Add three noises of your own.
2. What did he write about which makes you feel very quiet and still?
3. He noticed that some animals are hunters and that some always seem to be hunted. Write a list of animals which hunt, and a list of animals which get hunted. Begin with the ones that Richard mentions.

Richard Jeffries did not write very much about the things he noticed, but he watched and listened very carefully, and all the words he used are important. Here are some things for you to do after you have read the 'notes' again.

4. Richard watched a dog coming out of the water, and a baby as it sat down. Watch any animal or young child and see if you can write just as exactly about the way they move or do something.

5. The butterfly had wings like red velvet; what can you think of to say about the colour of:-

tree blossom, colour of ________

an old brick, colour of ________

a puddle, colour of ________

Anything else you like?

6. Thistledown and squirrels' fur are light and floaty and soft. Make a list of other things that feel rather like that. Can you say something about them?

TO DO AT HOME

- Get your notebook started. Jot down things that happen to you or things that you notice. Bring it to school fairly soon. This picture might give you some ideas.
- • Talk about the things that Richard Jeffries noticed. Which did you like best? Which have you seen?

Unit 3. Telling about happenings

Look back to the last unit where you read what Richard Jeffries said about what he saw. He noticed what people and animals did as well as what they looked like. You are going to tell about what happened to you last week. Use your notebook to help you remember. Even a little thing can be interesting if you tell exactly how it happened. Try to make a picture in your mind before you start talking.

• • In pairs Tell each other about some of the things in this list.

Something you enjoyed doing last week.
Something that made you laugh.
A time when you were frightened.
A time when you did something naughty.
A time when you felt sad.

Now join up with another pair.
Copy out the table below. Tick off what the four of you remembered. Put the ticks under the right headings.

Names	Happy	Funny	Frightening	Naughty	Sad
Total					

What things do you remember most as a group?

Make a tape-recording for the rest of the class where you tell about some of the things you talked about.

Now read what some other people have written about things that happened to them. The first three are by children. The Sparrow was written by Sarah Pearson.

> One Sunday our cat Smokey caught a little sparrow. He nearly killed it but we saved it. We dug up some worms and got a bowl of warm water. It ate a big fat juicy worm and it drank a little warm water. We got a little sawdust and we put the sparrow in the sawdust. We put it near the fire. We kept it warm, very warm. It flew round the room once. We took it outside to the bottom of the garden and it just dropped down. We ran to get it and took it back in again. It lived for another hour, then it died. We were very sad.

Stanley Gibson wrote about something that made him laugh.

> When I was small, one day I was at my aunty's she had a dog called Simon. The washing was on the line and my aunty's dog pulled a pair of knickers off the line and he would not give the knickers to my aunty.

Andrew Last felt rather sick.

Once my dad said, "Andrew, come on the roller coaster." I said I didn't want to, but my dad persuaded me and forced me. So I went on it and when it started I felt all funny inside and when we went down the hill I breathed in and closed my eyes and I thought the world was turning round and I felt I was upside down.

Dylan Thomas was a great writer. When he was grown up he wrote about his childhood. He remembered everything very clearly. Here is one of his memories.

And I remember that on the afternoon of Christmas Day, I would go out, with my bright new boots squeaking, to call on Jim and Dan and Jack. We went padding through the streets, leaving huge deep footprints in the snow, on the hidden pavements. We passed by Mr Daniel's house.

"Let's post Mr Daniel a snowball through his letter-box!"

"Let's write things in the snow."

"Let's write, 'Mr Daniel looks like a spaniel' all over his lawn."

"Look," Jack said, "I'm eating snow-pie."

"What's it taste like?"

"Like snow-pie," Jack said.

Try to notice where each writer talked about little things happening, very exactly. This makes it easier for us to picture it all in our minds.

Look at the pictures on pages 19, 20 and 21. Write down some words from each story which match the pictures.

Choose one hour next week and jot down all you can about what happened during that hour.

Like this:

FRIDAY 6 o'clock to 7 o'clock
Dog barked at paper-boy. Telly packed up. Bacon, egg and chips for tea. Lovely! Bored – no telly. Rained. Mum pleased with me – helped wash up.

Keep your notes safe for next time. You will need them.

Unit 4. Writing about events

LOOK IN YOUR NOTEBOOK

Find where you wrote down what you did for one hour.
Now you are going to find out how to write it so that it will be easy for other people to read. This means that you have to put it into sentences. You have to get things in the right order. You have to spell all the words right.
See how we have turned the notes from the last unit into a little story.

Last Friday I got home late from school. I was feeling very tired after a week's hard work. I thought I would have a rest and watch television till Mum had got my tea ready. Then everything	FRIDAY 6 o'clock to 7 o'clock
went wrong. My dog, Chum, rushed to the door, barking at the paper-boy. Chum caught hold of the paper as it came through the letter-box, and in a minute it was in a hundred bits. I switched	Dog barked at paper-boy.
the television on. Nothing happened.	Telly packed up.
I went into the kitchen. "What's the matter with you ?" said Mum. "Cheer up – you look like a wet week. Here's your favourite tea – bacon, egg and chips!"	Bacon, egg and chips for tea. Lovely!
I ate it up and felt a bit better. There wasn't much to do, though. There was no telly to watch, and it was raining too hard to go out to play.	Bored – no telly. Rained.
I helped wash up.	

Mum pleased with me – helped wash up.

"You *are* good," she said. "I'll take you shopping tomorrow." I felt much better then.

ONE THING LEADS TO ANOTHER

When you write for other people, it is important to get things in the right order. Here is the beginning of a book. The lines have got all mixed up, though. Try to write them out in the right order. The story is about a little boy called Treehorn, who thought he was growing smaller instead of bigger!

Then he noticed that his clothes were getting too big.

Something very strange was happening to Treehorn.

"That's too bad, dear," said his mother, looking into the oven.

"My trousers are all stretching or something," said Treehorn to his mother.

The first thing he noticed was that he couldn't reach the shelf in his closet that he had always been able to reach before.

"I'm tripping on them all the time."

The one where he hid his candy bars and bubble gum.

Can you write down which order these come in?

1

2

3

4

Nursery rhymes are easy to sort out into the right order. Can you write this one out?

Sat among the cinders

Warming her pretty little toes

Little Polly Flinders

For spoiling her nice new clothes

And whipped her little daughter

Her mother came and caught her

A MIX-UP

Find a nursery rhyme. Copy it out in large print on a piece of stiff paper. Leave plenty of room between each line. Rule a line between each line of the rhyme. Cut along the lines. Mix up the strips of paper so that they are in the wrong order. Give it to your friend. See if he or she can put it in the right order.

You might enjoy reading the book about Treehorn. It is called The Shrinking of Treehorn, by Florence Heide. It is published by Young Puffin Books.

Unit 5. Stories

In good stories there is always a part that you wait for because it is exciting. When you read a story you have to imagine what happened in the parts that are not in the book. You fill in the gaps for yourself. It is quite easy to guess.

Nursery rhymes are like very short stories. A lot has been left out. You can fill it in.

Here is a nursery rhyme that you know. You are going to think about what might have happened between the lines. Talk about each bit with your friend. Decide between you what the answers to the questions are. Write them down.
This is what Jack and Jill might look like.

Jack and Jill went for water.

Jack fell over.

Jill fell down too.

The first two lines:

Jack and Jill went up the hill
To fetch a pail of water.

1. Who do you think Jack and Jill were? Make up all you can about them.
2. Why were they going to get water?
3. Why was the water on a hill? Where did the water come from?

Now the next bit.

Jack fell down and broke his crown.

(That means bumped his head badly.)

A frog tripped them up.

4. Why do you think Jack fell down?
5. Had Jack and Jill already got the water when he fell down?

Now the last line.

And Jill came tumbling after.

6. Why did Jill fall down too?
7. Was she hurt?
8. How do you think it all ended?

Think of another nursery rhyme between you. See if you can make up some questions about the parts which are not explained. Give the rhyme and your questions to another pair of children to answer.

These are the pictures we have drawn for the story of Red Riding Hood. Picture 1 shows Red Riding Hood getting ready to go and see her grandma. Read the balloons and what is written underneath.

Find a story in a book that you enjoyed reading. It could be quite short, or a whole book.

Read your story carefully again. Choose the four parts which tell the most important happenings.
You are going to tell the story in pictures, making a cartoon strip. This is how you do it.

You need four cards to draw on.

Red Riding Hood is taking a present to Grandma.

Grandma looks very strange.

It is a wolf in Grandma's bed – not Grandma.

The woodcutter killed the wolf.

Draw one picture on each card. Each picture will tell the story of one bit. You can put balloons in for the words which the people in the picture might say. You can put one line of writing underneath each picture to say what it is about.

Now mix up the cards so that they are in the wrong order.

• • Change cards with your partner. Try to put the cards in the right order. You will need to read the story afterwards to see if you got it right.

Listen to your friends and the people at home talking. They often talk about things that made them laugh, or that frightened them, as you did last week. People make up stories about their lives.

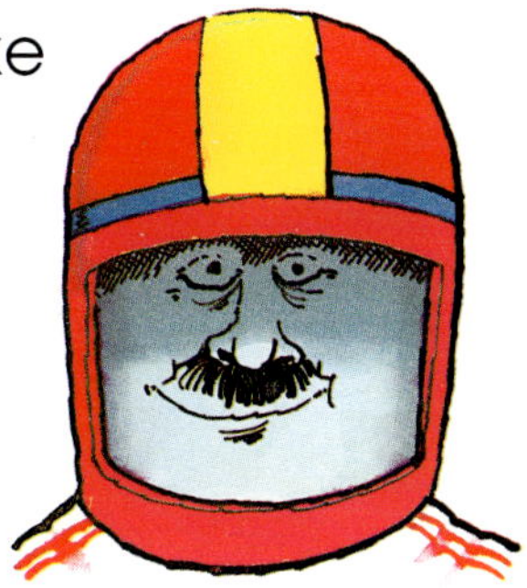

IN YOUR NOTEBOOK FOR NEXT TIME

Listen to people talking.

Try to write down some of the things they say.

You will not be able to get everything down. You may be able to write down some little things that they often repeat.

Listen carefully for what they say when they meet each other.

Listen to and write down what they say when they leave each other.

You will need this next time.

Unit 6. People talking

There are always people or animals in stories. They talk to each other. How can you tell if someone is talking when you are reading? Look at a book to see. There are little marks at the beginning of what each person says. “

Sometimes there is just one ‘

and at the end

Sometimes just one ’

Sometimes we call them sixty-sixes
and
ninety-nines ”

You can tell a lot about the people in stories from what they say. Many stories have animals talking in them. Of course, animals don't really talk. The writers have to make up what they think the animals would be saying.
A long time ago people told each other stories about animals who did very good things or very silly things. They are called fables.

Here are two animals from a fable. One is a lion. One is a hare.
The lion is much stronger and fiercer than the hare, but the hare is quick and clever. Read the words that they say to each other. You will be able to tell what the story is about from what they say. You are going to write their words down like a play. Copy out the parts of the Lion and the Hare. Put the name of the speaker in front of each speech. (The first two are done for you.)
You do not need 66's and 99's when you write a play.

Hare Oh, Mr Lion, what's the good of your eating me? I'm so small and thin! If you're hungry, I'll show you the way to a great fat beast. Only he is very strong. I'm afraid perhaps he might be too much for you.

Lion What? Too much for me! Is there any beast stronger than I? Show me this beast at once.

Oh, do be careful, and don't risk your life. You don't know what a terrible beast this is! And he lives at the bottom of a well.

Lead me to him at once!

You see what a terrible beast he is! You had better stop where you are, Mr Lion, and don't jump down into the well, or he'll tear you to pieces.

What? Do you think I'm afraid of him? I *will* jump into the well.

Oh, please don't!

Look at what Hare said. How can we tell that he is very clever?
What does he say to stop Lion eating him?
What does he say to make Lion show off and fall into his trap?
How does he catch Lion out?

Lion is rather stupid.
What does Lion say which shows that he thinks he is stronger than anyone?
What does Lion do which is not very clever?

How do you think the story might end?
Think of a clever way for Hare to save Lion, if he feels sorry for him.

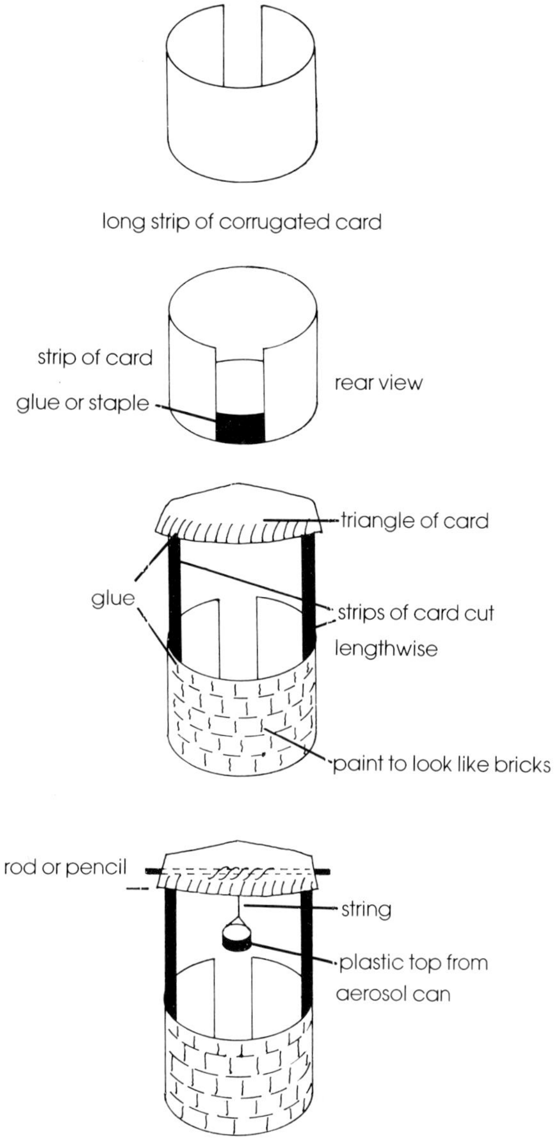

SOCK PUPPETS

Sock puppets are easy to make. Ask for old socks at home.
You can make the lion and the hare (like a big rabbit).

1. Crumple some newspaper and push it into the toe of the sock. Tie it round with string or an elastic band. That is the head.
2. Make the head look like your animal. Pin paper ears on the hare, make a mane out of wool for the lion. Sew on buttons for eyes. You can shape the nose by tying more string round. You can think of names for your two animals.
3. Put a cotton-wool tail on the hare and a long string tail on the lion.
4. Now put your hand and arm into the sock. You can move the head from inside. Find out how to open the animal's mouth by moving your fingers. Play with it for a bit to get used to it.

A PUPPET PLAY

You are going to make a puppet play. Follow all the instructions carefully.
Talk about the story. Where does it happen? How does it end?
Make some scenery. You will stand behind a blackboard or screen so that

only the puppets show. Fix a well so that the audience can see it.

Try out some special voices. You will want to put in roaring for the lion and squeaks for the hare. Make up more words if you want to.

Be sure you have agreed how the play is going to end. Is it a sad ending or a happy one?

Now act the play. Put the puppets on your hands and get used to them.

roar

squeak

groan

howl

rumble

mutter growl

mumble

splutter

Scene 1. Hare and Lion meet. Hare is scared, but he doesn't show it. Lion thinks he is very brave and strong. Talk to each other. Lion will probably move about a lot. Hare will be sure to get out of the way.

Scene 2. At the well. Make up words of your own. Try out the best way of making Lion fall in the well. You will need some sound effects.

Scene 3. What happens next? You will have to make up the whole of this scene, as it is not in the story. You can decide whether Hare is going to save Lion, or whether Lion finds a way out himself – or perhaps he never gets out?

When you have acted this story, you could make more puppets to act out other stories that you like.

LOOK IN YOUR NOTEBOOK

Find what you have written down where people are talking.
Some of your friends may have special sayings – words that they say as a habit, like "Great!" or "Brilliant!" or "Guess what?"
Your teacher may have phrases that she says nearly every day – like "Be quiet now children" or "Listen carefully" or "Very good try".
What about the people at home? See if you can make some lists of people you know and their favourite sayings.

There are 4 boxes on this page. Copy them on to paper.
Now fit these sayings into the right boxes.
To show you:
"Keep your ears skinned" means the same as "listen to what I am going to say", so you write it in box 2.

SAYINGS

Keep your ears skinned.	Great!
Get moving.	Guess what?
Stupendous!	Put your skates on.
Listen with all ears.	Keep your hair on.
Brilliant!	Speed it up a bit.
I haven't got all day.	Super-duper.
Temper! Temper!	Calm down.

Can you put some more sayings that you have heard in the boxes?

1. It is marvellous.

2. Listen to what I am going to say.

3. Hurry up.

4. Don't get cross.

Unit 7. Poems

Stories are good to read because exciting things happen. Stories are full of people and animals who do all sorts of things.
Poems can tell stories, but they are not so much about what people do, as about what they think and feel. Poems can make us feel happy or sad, or they can make us laugh.
Poets (the people who make poems up) think very carefully about the words they are using.
Here are some short poems with funny words in them.
Read them out loud. You can read them on your own or with someone else. Roll the words round your tongue.

There was an owl lived in an oak,
wisky, wasky, weedle;
And every word he ever spoke
Was fiddle, faddle, feedle.

Rub-a-dub-dub
Three men in a tub.

See-saw, Margery Daw

Rat-a-tat-tat, who is that?
Only Grandma's pussy cat.

The poems don't mean much. The words fit together well, though, and are fun to say. They are nursery rhymes for young children.
Here are some more.

Gregory Griggs, Gregory Griggs,
Had twenty-seven different wigs.

Rock, Rock, bubbly Jock,
Wake me up at ten o'clock.

Peter Piper picked a peck of pickled pepper;
Did Peter Piper pick a peck of pickled pepper?
If Peter Piper picked a peck of pickled pepper,
Where's the peck of pickled pepper Peter Piper picked?

Write out the nursery rhyme the artist has drawn.

Sometimes words sound like the noises that things make.

Can you make up some words to sound like these noises?

Read this aloud.

Clinkerdump, clankerdump, rattlecome ree

What do you think the words might be talking about? The next line tells you.

I live in the train and you can't see me.

Yes. The words in the first line sound like the wheels of the train going round.

Here's another poem. Copy it and fill in the word that has been missed out. (It's a word for 'rubber shoes'. If you can't guess, it comes in the next verse.)

Susie's ____________
Make splishes and sploshes
And slooshes and sloshes,
As Susie steps slowly
Along in the slush.

Here's the last verse. Copy it and fill in the words left out.

The slippery slush
As it slooshes and ____________
And ____________ and sploshes,
All round her galoshes!

Now you're going to make up your own. Do it this way unless you've already got some ideas of your own.

Here are some lists of words that begin with the same letter. (Some of them begin and end with the same letter.)

glig
glug
glog
glag

plip
plop
plap

tick
tock
tack

flip
flop
flap

Take one list of words. What does it make you think of?
Plip plop plap might make you think of rain. So you make a little rain poem. It might be like this.

Plip.
Plap.
The rain drops plop.
Rain go away.
Plap –
Plip – Plip – Plop –
STOP!

Now write down what the other groups make you think of.

In your group. Two of you read the poems you have made up aloud, while the other two tap out the beat on the desk, or on a drum, or with anything else that makes the right sort of noise.

AN ANTHOLOGY

Start your own anthology. This means that you copy all the poems that you come across into a book.

You can put ones you have made up in as well. You can draw pretty borders and pictures. You will want to keep the book for a long time, so make it look beautiful. You can collect funny rhymes as well. We will call the funny rhymes *play-poems*. You might hear them anywhere. In the playground or on TV.

Finder's keepers,
Loser's weepers.

Iddy, iddy onker,
My first conker.
Iddy, iddy ack,
My first smack.

BUILDING WITH WORDS

You can play with words.
They are rather like bricks.
Bricks are put together to make all sorts of different houses.
Words can be put together in different ways.
The same words can build different sentences.
Here are 6 words.

FLY BIRDS HIGH THE IN SKY

How would *you* build them into a sentence?

Here are 6 different ways.

1. Birds fly high in the sky.
2. High in the sky fly birds.
3. Fly, birds, high in the sky.
4. In the sky, birds fly high.
5. High birds fly in the sky.
6. In the high sky birds fly.

Each one means something a little different.

TRY THIS

Here are some words from a sort of play-poem about animals which live in sea-caves. The words are all mixed up together. Sort them out in any way you want to make a do-it-yourself poem. It is more fun if you copy every word on to a small piece of paper (one word for every piece). Then you can move the words around until you find what you like. You can miss out up to six words that you don't need. Copy out your poem when you have finished it.

caves of be and sea these

where or The

animals

and And snoozy grimy

the

Are animals slimy

and

grey the grey

Slim

safe

Look at your friend's poem. Is it anything like yours?

Now turn over and see how James Reeves put the words together. He was the poet who wrote it in the first place.

Whose poem did you like best? You can put all your poems in your anthology.

FOR NEXT TIME. IN YOUR NOTEBOOK

Listen when people tell you what to do. Write down what they say as exactly as you can.

Copy down any notices in the street and in shops which tell people what to do.

GRIM AND GLOOMY

Slim and slimy
or grey and grimy
Are the animals of the sea.
And safe and snoozy
The caves where these animals be.

by James Reeves

Unit 8. Instructions

What is important when you tell people to do something?
You have to say *exactly* what you want them to do.
You have to speak *clearly*.
You have to explain *simply*.
Try not to use too many words.
It is useful to say why you are asking them or telling them to do something.
Here are some instructions which a mother might give.
"Don't forget to clean your teeth." (She did not say when.)
"Turn the telly off now." (No getting round that. It is very clear.)
"Fetch my purse." (Not clear at all. She didn't say where it was.)

YOUR NOTEBOOK

Copy as many notices as you can which you have seen in streets, shops, hospitals, parks and other places.

Make two lists, like this:

Notices and signs which tell us things (information)	Notices and signs which tell us what we must not do (warnings)

Here are some to start you off.
GET YOUR SPUDS HERE.
NO OVERTAKING.
KEEP OFF THE GRASS.
DOGS MUST BE LED.

Which list is longer? Where would 'Beware of the dog' fit?

LOOK IN YOUR NOTEBOOK

Find the page where you jotted down where people gave instructions. (That means, told you to do something.) Are they clear?
You are going to write down 5 instructions to help children who are coming to school for the very first time. Remember what you found hard, and try to make it easier for them than it was for you. Put them into a list, 1–5.
Change your list with a friend, and see if you have thought of the same things.

There are all sorts of instructions in a school. This book gives you instructions. Most of your school books tell you how to do something. Copy out some of the instructions from different books. Put a tick by them if you think they are easy to follow, and a cross if they are difficult.

Sometimes you see signs without words. Draw as many of these signs as you can. Try to write down in words what they are telling us.

In the story of Winnie-the-Pooh, by A. A. Milne, Owl is the wisest animal in the wood. He lives in a tree. He has a door with a knocker. Here is a bit from the book.

Underneath the knocker there was a notice which said,
PLES RING IF AN RNSER IS REQIRD.
Underneath the bell-pull there was a notice which said,
PLEZ CNOKE IF AN RNSR IS NOT REQID.

What is silly about the notices?

A HUNDRED YEARS AGO

If you had lived a hundred years ago, you would have been given many instructions. Children were told exactly what to do and what not to do. If they did not do as they were told they got into trouble. Often they were punished. They were given stories to read which told them the terrible things that would happen to them if they did not obey their parents and teachers.

Here is one of the stories.

THE STORY OF LITTLE SUCK-A-THUMB

One day Mamma said, "Conrad dear,
I must go out and leave you here.
But mind now, Conrad, what I say,
Don't suck your thumb while I'm away.
The great tall tailor always comes
To little boys who suck their thumbs;
And ere they dream what he's about,
He takes his great sharp scissors out,
And cuts their thumbs clean off – and then
You know, they never grow again."

Mamma had scarcely turned her back,
The thumb was in, ALACK! ALACK!
The door flew open, in he ran,
The great, red-legged scissor-man,
Oh! children, see! the tailor's come
And caught out little Suck-a-Thumb,
Snip! Snap! Snip! the scissors go;
And Conrad cries out "Oh! Oh! Oh!"
Snip! Snap! Snip! They go so fast,
That both his thumbs are off at last.

Mamma comes home; there Conrad stands,
And looks quite sad, and shows his hands;
"Ah!" said Mamma, "I knew he'd come
To naughty little Suck-a-Thumb."

Parents tell their children what to do in different ways now. Here is a piece from a story by Betsy Byars, who is a writer from America. Lennie is a little boy who wants to watch TV all the time. His mum wants him to do his homework. Lennie does not take any notice for a long time.

> "Lennie, are you watching television?"
> "Lennie, I meant what I said about the television."
> "Lennie, go into my room right now and start studying."
> "Now!"
> Lennie's mother stopped in front of him. She turned off the television. As the picture faded to one small dot, she and Lennie looked at each other.
> "You've got to do your homework."
> "I'm going. I'm going."
> "You didn't have to do that," Lennie said. He was hurt. He felt as if his mother had slapped him.
> "You've got to do your homework."
> "Well, will you watch it for me?"
> "If you go right now."
> "I'm going. I'm going."
> "Len, will you please go into my room and start studying," Len's mum said tiredly. "I simply cannot argue with you this way every night."
> "I'm going."

Which of the two stories reminds you of yourself?

Make up either

A story about someone telling you what to do, and what happened,

or

A Cautionary Tale (like Little Suck-a-Thumb). You will have to think of a dreadful punishment. You do not need to make it rhyme.

Unit 9. Sharing opinions

Do you know what you like? Write down the answers to this quiz.

1. What is your favourite food?
2. What is your favourite drink?
3. What sort of clothes do you like wearing best?
4. What is your favourite game?
5. What is your favourite book?
6. What song do you like best?

Make up some more questions to ask your friends.

Now see how the others in the group have answered the quiz. Did you agree or disagree?

People think the same about some things, but nobody thinks exactly the same as another person about everything.
We have our own opinions.
It is good to find out what other people think. We may not agree, but we can still stay friends. We can listen to others and talk to them about what we like or don't like.

A PLAY

We are going to get to know the White family.

They have got to a place in the country for a picnic. Read this play about what happened when they arrived.

Mum Now come and sit over here, both of you children, where I can see you. I'm not running miles to find you. I soon get out of breath.

Mary I'm just going over to the pond. I want to see if there are any tadpoles. I won't be long.

Tommy I'm coming too! I'll help you get some, I've got a jar for them.

Mary I want to go on my own. Mum – tell Tommy to stay with you.

Grandad Now, no quarrelling, you two. I can't stand arguments.

Uncle John You can both come with me. I'll keep you in order. And I've got my fishing rod. You remember last time I was lucky?

Mum OK. While you're gone I'll put the picnic out. Here's the cloth to go on the grass – all nice and tidy.

Grandad Good. A bit of peace and quiet. Just time for a snooze. It's really hot here.

Mum Yes, but there's one of those awful buzzing things. Oh! It's got into a jam tart. Dad – *do* something!

Grandad All right. Keep calm. I'll get it out.

Mum Horrible gnats!

Grandad The proper name is mosquito. Here we are...

Mum Oh, don't kill it! I can't bear to see things killed.

Grandad One minute you're wanting to get rid of it and the next you're trying to stop me. You've always changed your mind a lot. You're getting worse in your old age.

Tommy (rushing back) Mum! Mary pushed me in the water and I'm all wet. She's horrible to me. I hate her!

Mum Oh dear, you're soaking! Where's the towel? In my bag. Lucky I think of everything. We mustn't have you catching cold. If you get a cold on your chest it always takes ages to go. Where's that naughty girl?

Mary (walking back) No tadpoles. Silly cry-baby. I didn't do anything to him, Mum.

Tommy Did.

Mary Didn't.

Grandad Now shut up, both of you. I came here for peace and quiet.

Mary What have we got to eat? Oh, goody, bacon butties. Oh, dear ... I've dropped it in the mud. That one will have to be for the birds.

Mum Oh, Mary! You're always so clumsy. Leave the food alone. Wait.

Mary (in a huff) I shall go back to Uncle John.

Mum No you don't. You stay right here.

Mary I'm off. Shan't be long.

Tommy (crying) I'm so cold and wet. I want to go home...

Uncle John and Mary come back.

Uncle John Look at my fish! I don't know what it's called. Where's my fishing book so I can look it up?

Grandad No need to look it up. I know. It's a tench. You never were one to remember names.

Mum (to Tommy) Here's a sausage, love, to keep you happy.

Tommy Don't like cold sausages.

Mum Have some lemonade, then.

Tommy Don't like lemonade. Only like Coke. (Sulks.)

Mary Let me help you, Mum. I like helping.

Mum You'll only drop everything. Leave it to me. Now here are the jellies.

Mary Oh, I love jelly! Can I eat mine now?

Grandad Don't be so impatient. You never wait for anything.

Mum Now isn't that lovely? The sun's shining, the picnic's ready, and we'll all enjoy ourselves.

Grandad I do like a bit of peace and quiet.

Uncle John Oh, good, my favourite – peanut butter sandwiches.

They begin to eat their picnic.

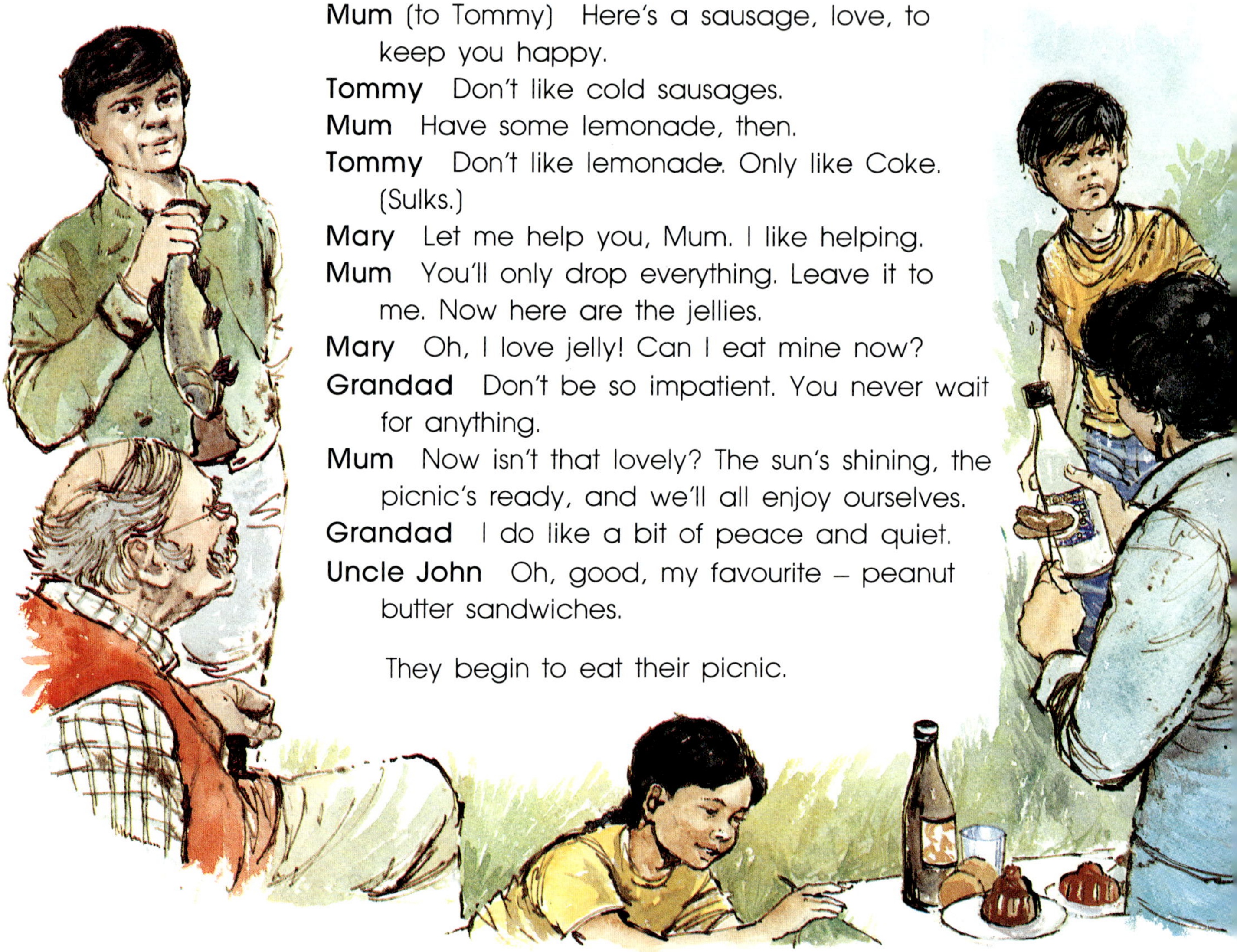

You can tell quite a lot about the people in this family, just by listening to what they say. You can tell about what they like and don't like.

Here are some mixed-up words and phrases which tell about their likes and dislikes.

The White family's likes and dislikes (mixed up)

running fast   exploring   helping
arguing   fishing   tidying up
peace   mosquitoes   killing insects
bacon butties   sausages
lemonade   coke   jelly
peanut butter sandwiches

Copy the table below and fill in the words where they belong. You might find some more to put in.

	LIKES	DOES NOT LIKE
GRANDAD		
MUM		
UNCLE JOHN		
MARY		
TOMMY		

You have probably got some idea about what sort of people they are, too. Here are some words which tell you this. They are all mixed up again. Some of the words might fit more than one of the White family. If so, you can use them twice when you fill in your table.

neat and tidy   adventurous   knows a lot
sleepy   kind   helpful   changeable
disobedient   quarrelsome   easily upset
clumsy   fussy   cheerful   sulky
impatient   calm   peace-loving   active

You may be able to add some of your own words.

Copy this table and fill in as you did before.

	WHAT SORT OF PERSON?
GRANDAD	
MUM	
UNCLE JOHN	
MARY	
TOMMY	

Compare your lists. Do you agree? Talk together about the family. Who do you think you would have got on with best?

A BOOK TO READ

The Battle of Bubble and Squeak, by Phillipa Pearce. This is a story about another family, the Sparrows – what they like and dislike and the sort of people they are.

Now write about someone in your family, or one of your friends. Say all you can about why you find them interesting, about what they like, and what they are like.

This is what David Grover wrote about his father.

I like him because he's a good laugh. He helps me a lot. For instance, he's going to start training me in the summer. He likes to drink but I've never known him drunk. My mum says I'm like him. We both like the same sport. If his back hadn't gone he would still be diving across the goal area. He has got blue eyes and long legs. He has got big shoulders. He likes to wear plain clothes. He is my dad.

Unit 10. Do you mean what you say?

People do not always mean what they say. Sometimes they exaggerate. They want to make what happened to them sound exciting. They add bits. They leave bits out. Sometimes people get cross and say things they don't really think.

Look back to the last unit and the White family's picnic.

Tommy says he hates Mary.

Mum says she thinks of everything.

Grandad says that Mary never waits for anything.

Mary calls Tommy a silly cry-baby.

They don't really mean these things. They are exaggerating.

Sometimes people exaggerate for fun, to make us laugh.

Here is a story which does that. Two hundred years ago, a man made up many adventures about Baron Munchhausen. The Baron was not a real man, but the writer made out that he was. He has fantastic adventures. Here is one of them.

The Baron was in a ship. He tells you what happened.

"A dreadful storm arose, which destroyed all our sails and broke the mast. We did not know where to steer. Then we began to see an amazing change in everything about us: we smelt a strange smell. The sea had changed from green to white! Soon after we saw land.

When we sailed up a wide river, we found it was made of milk of the most delicious taste. Here we landed, and soon found it was an island made of one large cheese. We found this out because one of the ship's crew fainted as soon as he landed. This man had always hated cheese. The people on this island live on the cheese. It grows during the night where it has been eaten during the day. Here there were plenty of vines, with bunches of big grapes. When we pressed them, milk ran out. The people who live here run races on the surface of the milk. They are good-looking people, nine feet

high. They have three legs and only one arm. When they quarrel, they wave a horn, which grows in the centre of their foreheads.

On this island of cheese grows plenty of corn, which produces loaves of bread, ready made, round like mushrooms. We found when we walked across the cheese, seventeen other rivers of milk, and ten of wine.

We found a great big bird's nest; it was at least twice the size of the dome of St. Paul's Church, in London. There were five hundred eggs in the nest. We managed to cut open one of the eggs. A young kingfisher came out, larger than twenty fully-grown eagles. Then the old kingfisher came to the nest. He got hold of our captain and flew with him a mile high, and then let him drop into the sea, but not till he had beaten all his teeth out of his mouth with his wings."

The artist has drawn some of the parts which could not possibly be true.

1. Write down the words which match the picture.
2. Write down 3 other parts which are not true.

That was what we call *a tall story.* There are short ones as well.
Here is a short tall story.

> He was so short that to get on his horse he had to stand on his head to get his foot in the stirrup.

And another

> I'm that unlucky that if it rained soup, everybody would have a spoon and I'd be left with a fork.

YOUR OWN TALL STORIES

You can make some of these up yourself.
To do it, you must be able to think of things in a different way from usual.
Try it like this.
Think of an ordinary thing, that you are used to seeing in one place.
Like a cup.
Where would you expect to find it?
Maybe

on a saucer.

Think of somewhere crazy to put it.

On a tree?

Write the sentence by your own picture.
I saw a cup hanging on a tree.

Now a cat.

Where would you expect to find it?

Maybe

on a wall.

Where shall we think of to put it?

In a swimming pool?

Think of some things with crazy places for yourself. Put your sentences together with your friends.

How many tall stories have you written?

You can play the game in a group. Decide on a thing, or a place. Between you think of all the crazy things you can to say about it. Make a group tall story. Draw pictures for every sentence and make a frieze to go round the classroom wall.

I saw a cat in a swimming pool.

Here is a poem about a bird which was in an unusual place.

SERGEANT BROWN'S PARROT

Many policemen wear upon their shoulders
Cunning little radios. To pass away the time
They talk about the traffic to them, listen to the news,
And it helps them to keep down crime.

But Sergeant Brown, he wears upon his shoulder
A tall green parrot as he's walking up and down
And all his parrot says is, "Who's-a-pretty-boy-then?"
"I am," says Sergeant Brown.

You might like some other poems by this writer, Kit Wright. His book of poems is called Rabbiting On.

Two silly rhymes to finish with. Can you say why they are silly?

I went to the pictures next Tuesday
And took a front seat at the back.
I said to the lady behind me,
I cannot see over your hat.
She gave me some well-broken biscuits,
I ate them and gave her them back,
I phoned for a taxi and walked it,
And that's why I never came back.

The elephant is a pretty bird,
It flits from bough to bough.
It builds its nest in a rhubarb tree
And whistles like a cow.

TO COPY AND FILL IN

MY CHECK LIST

Copy this check-list and fill it in

You will need your jotter, your neat work, and your Wordcraft book.

Fill in all the spaces that you can.

You may need more space if you have read a lot or written a lot.

You may have to leave some spaces if you have not done the activities.

When you have finished, ask your teacher to sign it in the right-hand column.

I have worked from Wordcraft Book 1 from ______ to ______ (dates)

Teacher's signature

WHAT I HAVE WRITTEN

1. My notebook

   I have filled ______________ pages (How many?)

2. Other writing

   I have written these poems.
   Put their names. ______________

____

____

I have made lists about: ______________

____

____

I have written instructions for: ______________

____

____

I have written these stories (or plays). ______________
Put their names. ______________

____

I have started an anthology. ______________
The names of the three poems I like best are: ______________

____

____

WHAT I HAVE DONE WITH SOMEONE ELSE

Teacher's signature

Put the names of children you worked with if you can remember.

____

____

I have **talked about** Put ticks or crosses
Sounds (page 5)
What happened to us (page 18)
Our families (page 54)

I have **played**
The whispering game (page 8)
Mystery object (page 13)
Putting nursery rhymes in order (page 25)

I have **made**
A cartoon-strip story (page 28)
Puppets (Unit 6)

I have **made up**
A quiz (page 49)
Tall stories (page 59)

WHAT I HAVE READ

Teacher's signature

Did you get these books to read?

The Surprise Party
The Shrinking of Treehorn
Winnie-the-Pooh
The TV Kid
Rabbiting On

Put the names of other books that you have enjoyed.

____

____

WHAT I HAVE LEARNT

Put a tick or a cross by each sentence.

I know what a question is.
I know what a story is.
I know what a play is.
I know what a poem is.
I know what instructions are.
I know when you use quotation marks (" ")

Which part of the book did you enjoy most?

Was there anything you did not enjoy doing?
What was it?

ACKNOWLEDGEMENTS

The author and publishers wish to thank the following copyright owners for permission to quote from copyright works.

Page 8: The extract from *The Surprise Party* is reproduced by permission of The Bodley Head; page 11: 'Summer night' and 'Is it a shower of rain?' from *The Penguin Book of Japanese Verse* are reproduced by permission of Penguin Books; page 19: 'The Sparrow' by Sarah Pearson, page 20: 'When I was small...' by Stanley Gibson and 'Once my Dad said...' by Andrew Last are from *A Second Suffolk Schools Anthology* edited by Helen Arnold; page 21: The extract from *Memories of Childhood* by Dylan Thomas, published by J M Dent is reproduced by permission of David Higham Associates Ltd; page 24: from *Shrinking of Treehorn* by Florence P Heide published by Young Puffin; page 39: 'Susie's Galoshes' by Rhoda BacMeister, from *Stories to Begin On* published by E P Dutton & Co; page 44: 'Grim and Gloomy' from *The Wandering Moon* by James Reeves is reprinted by permission of William Heinemann Ltd; page 48: The extract from *The TV Kid* by Betsy Byars is reproduced by permission of Bodley Head; page 46: the extract from *Winnie-the-Pooh* by A A Milne is reproduced by permission of Methuen; page 54: 'I like him because...' by David Grover from *A Second Suffolk Schools Anthology* edited by Helen Arnold; page 60: 'Sergeant Brown's Parrot' from *Rabbiting On* by Kit Wright published by Fontana Paperbacks.

Pages 6 and 7: the cartoons by Norman Thelwell from *Top Dog* are reproduced by permission of Methuen London; page 46: the line illustration by E H Shepard, copyright under the Berne Convention, is reproduced by permission of Curtis Brown Ltd, London.

Drawings
Douglas Clark: pages 8–9
Jane Cope: pages 10, 11, 14, 15, 16, 17, 24, 25, 37, 38, 39, 40, 41, 55, 56, 57, 58, 59
Tony Morris: page 4
David Mostyn: pages 5, 18, 19, 22, 23, 26, 27, 28, 29, 30, 33, 44
Trevor Parkin: pages 3, 13, 21, 49, 50, 51, 52

Photographs
Iona Cruikshank: pages 3, 34, 35
Camera Press: page 20

Design
Douglas Clark

ISBN 0 00 313009 6

Published by Collins Educational, London and Glasgow
Printed in Italy by
Tipolitografia G. Canale & C. S.p.A – Torino
in association with Keats European Limited

The puppets on pages 33 and 34 were made by children at St. Augustine's School in Salford.